HERMIT CRAB

Every Detailed Thing You Need To Know About The Hermit Crab. How To Feed, breed, House And Take Good Care Of Your Hermit Crab

VINCENT GLENN

Table of Contents

CHAPTER ONE

INTRODUCTION

Hermit crabs are omnivorous scavengers, eating microscopic mussels and clams, bits of dead animals, and microalgae.

These crustaceans had been misnamed for two reasons: First, they're not genuine crabs, like blue crabs, in that they don't have a uniformly difficult exoskeleton and can't grow their very own shells. rather, hermit crabs have a hard exoskeleton on the front a part of their bodies but a soft tail on the alternative half, which they shield using the discarded shells of other animals, like whelks. They're more intently associated with sure sorts of lobsters than to true crabs.

Hermit crabs have a curled tail with a hook that allows their bodies to in shape inside these borrowed shells. Once in a while when a new shell turns up, hermit crabs will form a line, biggest to smallest, to see which animal fits the brand new shell. The subsequent smallest will take that crab's hand-me-down home, and so on.

This conduct of sheltering in shells alone is honestly what gives them their call. But hermit crab is a misnomer for these social crabs, which on occasion live in huge corporations of 100 or greater within the wild.

CHAPTER TWO

HOW HERMIT CRAB MATE AND MULTIPLY

Hermit crabs vary of their mating conduct. The Caribbean hermit crab, as an example, lives in wetlands, however while it's time to mate, will head for the beach in large loads.

Amid the chaos, women and men locate each other, coming partially out of their shells so the male can transfer a sperm packet to the lady, which fertilizes her eggs. She later incorporates her eggs to the water's facet, where touch with seawater causes the eggs to burst and the larvae to flow away.

The larval crabs will stay on ocean plankton, molting thru several ranges earlier than obtaining a shell of their personal and coming again to land.

Hermit crabs don't breed properly in captivity, and so the numerous land hermit crabs seen in pet stores and traveler shops are taken from the wild, that's taken into consideration an unsustainable practice.

Plastic pollution is also a hassle for hermit crabs, which often mistake a plastic bottle cap or box for a new domestic. Whilst these trapped crabs die, they launch a pheromone signal to other crabs that there may be a shell available, which lures even more crabs into a loss of life lure.

CHAPTER THREE

HOW TO SET UP A SAND TANK FOR HERMIT CRAB

Hermit crabs do not want a complex domestic, but an appropriate temperature and humidity are crucial to their health. Land hermit crabs come from heat tropical climates and, consequently, they need a warm, humid environment to continue to exist.

Selecting the Tank

Hermit crabs will experience at home in either a glass or plastic tank. Pick out a 10-gallon aquarium with a lid. A sliding glass one will work nicely to contain humidity. The small plastic houses with add-ons sold as hermit crab kits are too small, even though those plastic cages make exceptional transient homes or isolation tanks. No matter their call, hermits are quite social and are excellent saved in agencies.

Substrate

Sand is the substrate of choice for hermit crabs due to the fact they prefer to burrow down into it. Playground sand, which may be located at home development shops, works nicely and is inexpensive, although aquarium sand is quality as properly. You may want to rinse, dry, and bake the sand (at 300 levels Fahrenheit) to sterilize it, and it is able to be rewashed and used once more. Calcium-primarily based sands are fine and come in a big selection of colors but are highly-priced.

Different alternatives consist of fiber bedding made for reptiles inclusive of the coconut fiber-based bedding referred to as wooded area Bedding. The fiber is floor pretty nice and is sort of like soil, so it is right for burrowing.

Crushed coral is likewise a pleasant preference, but you may need to offer an area with wooded area Bedding or sand as your hermit crabs may additionally pick these substrates for molting. Keep away from the usage of gravel or wood shavings.

Preserving right Temperature

Hermit crabs are happiest kept at seventy 2 to 8 ranges Fahrenheit (22 to 27 levels Celsius). If the temperature drops beneath 72 levels Fahrenheit regularly, the crabs will in all likelihood ends up susceptible, stressed, and ill. Until you live in a tropical climate, you will want to use a heater at the least part of the time to hold the crab tank at optimum temperatures. Under tank warmers (UTHs), lighting, or an aggregate of both can be used to hold suitable temperatures.

The UTHs may be located beneath one end of the tank to provide a heat facet and a cooler aspect. These will increase the temperature some degrees above room temperature. For best temperature manage, these can be combined with a thermostat to keep a given temperature, or you may place them on a timer to come back on and rancid to preserve temperatures. Spend money on a great thermometer for inside the tank, and screen the temperature near the substrate. If the heater is not heating the tank enough, strive casting off a number of the substrates over the heater—the thinner substrates will growth the warmth inside the tank. If the tank is getting too warm, you may growth the depth of the substrate. Some experimentation can be vital to get desirable, strong temperatures. Ensure that there is a temperature gradient in the tank, so the crabs have a preference of temperatures.

Lights of numerous sorts also can offer warmness for the tank; some experimentation with lights will also be vital to find the aggregate of lighting fixtures and UTH that works high-quality for your tank.

Lighting fixtures

Inside the past, it changed into concept that hermit crabs had been nocturnal and that offering lighting will be stressful for the crabs. but, low-wattage and unique night time light bulbs are a terrific choice, and plenty of crab owners have determined their crabs became extra active with lighting or even bask close to the lighting when the lighting fixtures become added to the tank. Make certain to provide a mild-darkish cycle, together with 12 hours of mild and 12 hours of darkish. This indicates day-glow or fluorescent bulbs have to only be off at night, although unique middle of the night bulbs may be used if desired. Using a desk lamp to warmth the tank, or excessive-wattage reptile bulbs, may also overheat the tank and be too drying, so those aren't encouraged.

The very best manner to feature lighting fixtures is to apply a reptile heating/lighting fixtures hood over the tank. Hoods can be determined with ceramic receptacles for incandescent bulbs; a day-glow bulb can be placed on one aspect and a night glow bulb within the other. Its miles high-quality to begin with 15-watt bulbs and go to higher wattages handiest if necessary, mainly with a ten-gallon tank. If important, wooden slats can be used to elevate the hood a bit above the glass if it receives too hot. Reptile heat hoods are exceptional used on glass pinnacle tanks or monitors, even though display screen tops make humidity law difficult, because the lights can be quite warm and could soften the plastic.

An aggregate of lights and under tank heat may be used to warmness the tank.

Humidity

In conjunction with the proper temperature, adequate humidity within the tank is vitally essential to hermit crabs. Due to the fact crabs "breathe" thru gills, the right trade of oxygen by the crabs depends on the humidity inside the air. If the tank air is too dry, the crabs will essentially suffocate. They need a relative humidity of around 70 to eighty percentage. Due to the fact this is so critical to the crabs, its miles worth investing in a humidity meter, known as a hygrometer, which you may locate inside the reptile section of the puppy store. Extra humidity isn't suited either because it will reason condensation in addition to encouraging the growth of bacteria and fungus inside the tank.

The water dish you offer inside the tank will probably be enough for growing the right humidity, so long as the tank is enclosed with solid facets and pinnacle. In case you need to growth the humidity degree, attempt a reasonably massive bite of a herbal sea sponge in a dish of water (do not forget to always use dechlorinated water).

The sponge can hold masses of water and has plenty of floor for evaporation to enhance the humidity. Have more than one sponge handy so you can change and clean them frequently (soak them in very hot dechlorinated water or a sea salt/water mix, then permit them to dry absolutely as they may be an amazing medium for bacterial growth). If a mesh or vented lid is making humidity control tough, the lid may be modified by means of masking maximum of the pinnacle with plastic wrap or clean packing tape.

CHAPTER FOUR

SETTING UP A CAGE FOR YOUR HERMIT CRAB

There are 3 necessities for furnishing the cage: stuff to climb on, a water bowl, and meals dish.

• Hiking: Land hermit crabs love to climb, and this is a great manner to offer some workout. Choya (or cholla) wooden is good and may be arranged to permit climbing. Portions of coral, driftwood, and other sorts of wooden can be used—the reptile section of the puppy save is a great region to look for a variety or test the net hermit crab stores listed underneath. Artificial floras also are a extraordinary addition to the crab tank. Periodically alternate matters around or add different objects to provide some variety and interest for the crabs

•   Water: Hermit crabs have to have got right of entry to both sparkling and saltwater, so you will need water dishes. They need to be big and deep sufficient to allow the crabs get into them in the event that they wish to soak—mainly the saltwater dish—however clean to get out of and now not so deep that drowning is a chance. Strawberry hermit crabs must accept a salt pool deep enough to absolutely submerge themselves in, however for maximum species, it does not need to be that deep. With deeper dishes, smooth river stones or pieces of coral may be used as ramps or steps for the crabs to get out of the water. You must additionally vicinity natural sea sponges inside the water dishes; some crabs will press on those to get water to drink, and they help modify the humidity. All water given to the hermit crabs or used inside the tank need to be dechlorinated (the drops to be had at puppy shops). Saltwater have to be organized the usage of a marine aquarium salt such as an immediate ocean (mix as for saltwater tanks), no longer the salt made for freshwater tanks and never desk salt.

• Meals: For food dishes, you may need something shallow, sturdy, and smooth-to-easy. Flattened heavy plastic dishes made to appear like rocks can be found inside the reptile section, or you can use shallow ceramic dishes made for small animals. a few humans additionally use herbal sea shells for feeding.

- Feeding Hermit Crabs

In the wild, land hermit crabs are omnivore that means they eat both plant and animal remember. In captivity, their eating regimen should be primarily based on a balanced business food supplemented with a spread of sparkling foods and treats.

CHAPTER FIVE

FOOD AND TREATMENT TO GIVE YOUR HERMIT CRAB

Even as the economic diets are convenient and most are pretty well balanced, they must be supplemented with fresh meals. Hermit crabs appear specifically fond of having a varied weight loss plan. An extensive form of meals from the list below ought to be offered on a rotating foundation (a few each day, then a handful of others the subsequent, and so forth).

Sparkling meals and treats you could strive include

- Mango

- Papaya

- Coconut (sparkling or dried)

- Apples

- Applesauce

- Bananas

- Grapes

- Pineapple

- Strawberries

- Melons

- Carrots

- Spinach

- Watercress

- Leafy green lettuces (no longer iceberg/head lettuce)

- Broccoli

- Grass

- Leaves and strips of bark from deciduous timber (no conifers)

- Nuts (unsalted nuts)

- Peanut butter (occasionally)

- Raisins

• Seaweed (found in some fitness meals and grocery stores for wrapping sushi)

• Crackers (no or low salt)

• Unsweetened cereals

• Undeniable rice desserts

• Popcorn (simple, air popped, can be given every now and then)

• Cooked eggs, meats and seafood (moderately)

• Freeze dried shrimp and plankton (found in the fish meals section at the pet keep)

• Brine shrimp

• Fish food flakes

This listing isn't always exhaustive as different comparable meals may be fed as well. Quite tons any fruit (clean or dried) can be presented, despite the fact that some experts recommend heading off noticeably acidic or citrus meals (e.g. oranges, tomatoes). Attempt a diffusion of veggies however avoid starchy vegetables such as potatoes and live far from iceberg lettuce as it's far of very low dietary cost. Crabs may also without a doubt like salty, fatty, or sugary snacks which include pretzels, chips, and sweetened cereal but these must be averted.

Meals and Water Dishes

For food dishes, you may need something shallow, robust, and smooth to clean. Flattened heavy plastic dishes made to seem like rocks can be observed within the reptile phase, or you could use shallow ceramic dishes made for small animals. A few humans additionally use herbal sea shells (the flatter half shells) for feeding.

Seeing that all species of hermit crabs need to have get admission to each fresh and salt water, you will want two water dishes. They ought to be big and deep sufficient to allow the crabs get into them if they desire to soak (specifically the salt water dish), however smooth to get out of and no longer so deep that drowning is a chance (strawberry hermit crabs should accept a salt pool deep enough to absolutely submerge themselves in, however for maximum species it does now not need to be that deep). With deeper dishes, clean river stones or pieces of coral can be used as ramps or steps for the crabs to get out of the water.

33

THE END

www.ingramcontent.com/pod-product-compliance
Lightning Source LLC
Chambersburg PA
CBHW051407150726